MW00568934

Especially for

_____

From

_____

Date

_____

© 2011 by Barbour Publishing, Inc.

ISBN 978-1-61626-199-3

Compiled by Patricia Lutherbeck and Susan Duke in association with Snapdragon Group℠, Tulsa, OK.

Published by Barbour Publishing, Inc., P.O. Box 719, Uhrichsville, Ohio 44683, www.barbourbooks.com

Our mission is to publish and distribute inspirational products offering exceptional value and biblical encouragement to the masses.

Member of the
Evangelical Christian
Publishers Association

Printed in China.

Sometimes, a

WOMAN

Just Knows. . .

BARBOUR
PUBLISHING

A woman can smell mink through
six inches of lead.

GROUCHO MARX

Spending just one evening with your girlfriends can erase a whole week of bad days.

Unlike your male counterparts,
no one will condemn you for
staying home to raise the kids.

Chocolate really can
make the world
a better place.

Real women cry.
A lot.

You'll never be too old to
fly a kite, gaze at the stars,
or walk in the rain.

Telling a woman she "can't"
is all the motivation she needs
to prove she "can."

Men work; but women work,
grocery shop before they head home,
fix dinner, clean the house, do the laundry,
and take care of the children.

Pantyhose and underwire bras
were originally created as
ancient torture devices.

Asking for directions
when you're lost is
a no-brainer.

I am woman! I am invincible! . . .
I am exhausted!

There are a million reasons to be happy you're a woman—shoe shopping, girls' nights, and cheaper insurance (just to name a few).

A woman can be delicate and refined. . .or capable of the most masculine tasks.

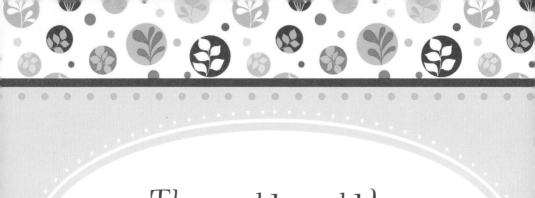

The world would be
a colder, harsher place
if not for women.

As long as you throw a box of tampons into the mix, no one will judge you for the multiple bars of chocolate, half-gallon of ice cream, jar of chocolate fudge, and can of whipped topping you are purchasing!

I'd much rather be a woman than a man. Women can cry, they can wear cute clothes, and they are the first to be rescued off sinking ships.

GILDA RADNER

If men were left to their own devices, they would starve to death.

Nothing can compare to the female body's ability to harbor a growing life and produce the food to feed it after it is born.

Chocolate is a food group!

Just because you're a woman
doesn't mean you have to get married.

Women have the ability to make something delicious out of a refrigerator of leftovers.

You can be a ballerina
or a race car driver—
the possibilities
are limitless.

Your closet offers you the opportunity to re-create yourself, just by choosing a different outfit.

Smiling is the best
beauty regime of all.

You have the freedom to change
your hair color as often as you like.

What you are on the inside is more important than what you look like on the outside.

Finding your favorite shade of lipstick when you thought it had been discontinued can give you a whole new lease on life.

Secretly, men *know* that women rule the world.

If you want something done right,
you will probably have to do it yourself.

Although you like being taken care of, you are totally capable of taking care of yourself.

You are not defined by
your marital status.

Having girlfriends to share
life with keeps you sane.

What you don't like about your body
can always be hidden with makeup,
clothes, and specialty undergarments.

Your beauty should not come from
outward adornment, such as elaborate
hairstyles and the wearing of gold jewelry
or fine clothes. Rather, it should be that
of your inner self, the unfading beauty
of a gentle and quiet spirit, which is of
great worth in God's sight.

1 PETER 3:3–4 NIV

Spending ten minutes talking to a total stranger in the checkout line at the grocery store is completely normal.

As a woman you are expected to,
and probably will, cry at all weddings and births.

If you are looking for an honest opinion about your outfit, *never* ask a man!

Fool me once, shame on you.
Fool me twice, you had
better start running!

Clothes are more than just a way to cover your body; they are a well-considered statement about who you are.

Brains will take you farther
in life than beauty.

You can be strong and sensitive at the same time.

Sending a child off to school
for the first time usually requires
a visit to the therapist's office.

You are not a trophy, but a precious gift
to be honored and cherished.

You know, men and women are a lot alike in certain situations. Like when they're both on fire—they're exactly alike.

DAVE ATTELL

If you don't look out for yourself,
no one else will.

Even a small bouquet
of flowers can turn your
whole day around.

Being a good "role" model is by far
a greater accomplishment than
being a good "fashion" model.

Life is like the weather:
give it a little time,
and it will change.

Perfect housekeeping is overrated.

You can accomplish anything
you set your heart and mind to do.

God created you by design
to be a mysterious creature
(that men can never figure out!).

Never reveal where you
keep your chocolate stash.

Occasionally you need to slow down and take some time to smell the roses.

Laughing with a girlfriend is better than a doctor's prescription.

There are three things in life you can't live without: faith, hope, and love.

If you have to ask,
the answer is probably "no."

Whoever said that life is a continual
feast wasn't doing the cooking.

Depression is easily conquered with one of two things: chocolate or Mexican food.

When it's time to toss the superwoman
cape, grab a pair of reading glasses,
a tall glass of iced tea, and relax
with a good book.

Hearts and china
are both easily broken.

Attitude is a choice. You can cry over a red sock accidently tossed into a wash load of white clothes. . .or smile and realize you have created a beautiful shade of pink.

You must choose your battles wisely.

Every wrinkle has a story to tell.

*A good woman is hard to find
and worth far more than diamonds...
She's quick to assist anyone in need,
reaches out to help the poor.*

PROVERBS 31:10, 20 MSG

When absolutely necessary, you can tackle most any home repair job with hair spray, a high heel, a rubber band, WD-40, and duct tape.

It's the little daily and unexpected surprises that matter most.

Happiness, at any given moment,
often depends on your caffeine intake.

You always know when a little self-care, pampering, or a spa day is long overdue!

Your heart will feel lighter after you've shed a few tears.

Some bathing suits can be
hazardous to your health!

Life is too short
to wear high heels.

You came equipped with radar that alerts you when something's not quite right.

Wild horses couldn't drag a secret out of most women. However, women seldom have lunch with wild horses.

IVERN BOYETT

Music is as important to housecleaning as a dust cloth.

Pretending to like sports is one of the keys
to a successful marriage.

If you want your teenager to do something, all you have to do is tell her not to.

Talking is a hobby.

If it involves roses,
the answer is "yes."

You *will* laugh about this someday.

Someone always gets hurt.

A kindhearted woman gains respect.

PROVERBS 11:16 NIV

Sure God created man before woman. But then you always make a rough draft before the final masterpiece.

UNKNOWN

When dealing with children, bribery works!

If something can go wrong, it will.

If you wait until you're ready,
you will never do it.

Some part of you will always be a little girl.

It is possible to pack a week's worth of clothes
for a family of four into one suitcase.

Despite what "other people" might
have you believe, you *are* always right.

Dieting is for the birds.

It is impossible to please everyone
all of the time.

When all else fails,
there is ice cream.

The best mini-vacation
is a hot bubble bath.

Your best and most cherished snapshots
are memories of the heart.

Living life with gratitude
creates an awareness
of daily blessings.

Your family and friends are
your greatest treasures.

Treating yourself to a pedicure makes the whole world seem a bit rosier.

The hardest years in life are
those between ten and seventy.

HELEN HAYES

A compliment is more energizing
than a B-12 shot.

You have the power to encourage,
shape, and change lives.

Real faith grows
in the dark.

Buying bread feeds your body;
buying flowers feeds your soul.

Growing older with grace
is easier said than done.

Dieting could be hazardous
to your mental health.

A little retail therapy is always more
fun when shared with a friend.

Anything tastes better when
you add Velveeta cheese.

Your purse holds most
everything you need—
and doubles as a weapon
if needed.

A man who will wear an apron
also wears an invisible halo.

Although a tomato is technically a fruit,
you won't be tossing one in a fruit salad.

Life is filled with small
puzzle-piece glimpses
of the total picture.

A confident attitude is your best accessory.

You are the heroine of your
own romance story.

It is your prerogative
to change your mind
as often as you like.

The only smart diet is the
one you haven't gone on yet.

My second favorite household chore is ironing;
my first being hitting my head on the
top bunk bed until I faint.

ERMA BOMBECK

Sooner or later you will turn into your mother, and there isn't a thing you can do about it.

There is absolutely nothing wrong with being a strong and independent woman.

The more *you* pretend to like
your husband's friends,
the more *he* will not.

Good communication is the
key to any relationship.
Lack of communication will
kill a relationship for sure.

You deserve to be pampered,
even if you have to
do it yourself!

Your life is constantly evolving,
and you will need to roll with the changes.

On cool evenings,
the porch swing really is
calling your name.

With every new sunrise,
new blessings are on the way.

You have to stop wishing and take that first step to jump-start your dreams!

It takes another woman
to really understand
your questions.

You were born a female; therefore, you *will* talk to your friends about everything.

Charm is deceptive, and beauty is fleeting; but a woman who fears the LORD is to be praised. Honor her for all that her hands have done, and let her works bring her praise at the city gate.

PROVERBS 31:30–31 NIV

You are not defined
by the house you keep.

Someday your prince will come.
He may not be royalty, but he will come.

You can speak baby talk
to a stranger's infant,
and no one thinks you're weird.

Women are not the weak, frail little flowers that they are advertised. There has never been anything invented yet, including war, that a man would enter into, that a woman wouldn't, too.

WILL ROGERS

All you need is to hear
that you are loved.

God sometimes uses people
to answer prayers.

Tomorrow is the first day
of the rest of your life.

There are two ways to the heart of every man—his stomach and his family.

Those dishes aren't going
to wash themselves.

The treasures of your
heart are as unique as
your fingerprints.

Stars are God's way of reminding
you to keep on shining.

A dining room table just doesn't look right without flowers.

The perfect man doesn't exist,
but there are a few that come
pretty close.

No matter how small your contribution
to life may be, you should give it
with your whole heart.

You have the ability to reinvent
yourself with just one
$10 box of hair color.

You possess enough courage
to tackle any obstacle
that comes your way.

Your future is not
defined by your past.

If you forgot to pack it,
you can bet you will need it.

The greener grass on the other side
of the fence is usually just Astroturf.

If a man seems too good to be true,
he probably is.

A woman's mind is cleaner than a man's—
that's because she changes it more often.

OLIVER HEREFORD

Women all know. . .the absolute
moment when *enough is enough!*

You will never be perfect,
and it's okay.

There is beauty all around you if you will only slow down enough to appreciate it.

Your dream won't become reality without a fight and a commitment to hard work.

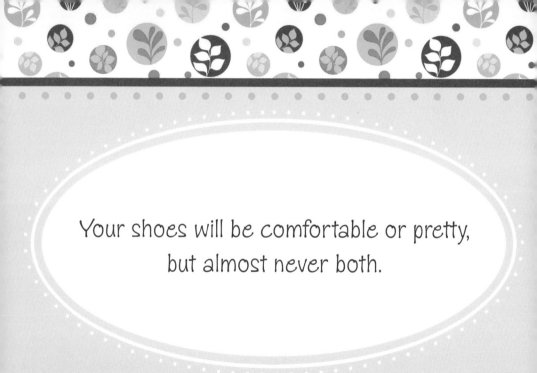

Your shoes will be comfortable or pretty,
but almost never both.

You must never stop believing
in your "happily ever after."

You should be willing to
accept people as they are,
but know when to walk away.

You must have a "happy place" and visit it often—your sanity depends on it.

The only standards you need
to uphold are your own.

Always have a back-up plan.

If you want to be loved,
you must first love yourself.

Knights in shining armor
are an endangered species.

Not only can you bring home the bacon, but you can also turn it into a delicious meal in thirty minutes or less.

Your femininity is not defined
by your physical assets.

You will not live your life
restrained by gender stereotypes.

Whatever women do, they must do twice as well as men to be thought half as good.... Luckily, this is not difficult.

CHARLOTTE WHITTON

You *can* and *will* change your
mind a million times.

Without women, men's lives
would be very, very dull.

You have the option of
more than one hairstyle.

Love makes the world go around.

Your versatility as a female is rivaled by none. Gardening, sports, children, and rocket science—the list goes on. You can do it all.

Stores are filled with thousands of items that cater to your female needs.

Despite your soft exterior,
you are tough enough to take on any
challenge that comes your way.

Being a woman is the greatest gift
God has given you.